WITHDRAWN

THOMAS JEFFERSON

CAROL H. BEHRMAN

**In Consultation with Martha Cosgrove,
M.A. and Reading Specialist**

HUNTINGTON CITY-TOWNSHIP
PUBLIC LIBRARY
200 W. Market Street
Huntington IN 46750

JUST THE FACTS BIOGRAPHIES

LERNER PUBLICATIONS COMPANY/MINNEAPOLIS

This book about a great American is dedicated to my beloved children—Bonnie, Joe, and Linda.

Martha Cosgrove has a master's degree from the University of Minnesota in secondary education, with an emphasis on developmental and remedial reading. She is licensed in 7–12 English and language arts, developmental reading, and remedial reading. She has had several works published, and she gives numerous state and national presentations in her areas of expertise.

Copyright © 2006 by Carol H. Behrman

All rights reserved. International copyright secured. No part of this book may be reproduced, stored in a retrieval system, or transmitted in any form or by any means—electronic, mechanical, photocopying, recording, or otherwise—without the prior written permission of Lerner Publishing Group, except for the inclusion of brief quotations in an acknowledged review.

Lerner Publications Company
A division of Lerner Publishing Group
241 First Avenue North
Minneapolis, Minnesota 55401 U.S.A.

Website address: www.lernerbooks.com

Library of Congress Cataloging-in-Publication Data

Behrman, Carol H.
    Thomas Jefferson / by Carol H. Behrman.
        p.   cm. — (Just the facts biographies)
    Includes bibliographical references (p.   ) and index.
    ISBN-13: 978-0-8225-2645-2 (lib. bdg. : alk. paper)
    ISBN-10: 0-8225-2645-X (lib. bdg. : alk. paper)
    1. Jefferson, Thomas, 1743–1826—Juvenile literature. 2. Presidents—United States—Biography—Juvenile literature. I. Title. II. Series.
    E332.79.B44 2006
    973.4'6'092—dc22   2005013165

Manufactured in the United States of America
1 2 3 4 5 6 – BP – 11 10 09 08 07 06

CONTENTS

CHAPTER 1

A BOYHOOD ON THE PLANTATION

Jefferson *(above right)* spent hours writing the Declaration of Independence. This painting shows him reading his first draft to Benjamin Franklin *(above left)*.

THOMAS JEFFERSON sat at a desk in his second-floor room on a July day in 1776. He was thirty-three years old. The chair and desk were small for his tall frame, but he was too busy to notice. His pen moved across the page, trying to keep up with his thoughts. He scratched out words and phrases as he thought of better ones.

Every so often, he stood up to stretch. From the window, he saw the busy city of Philadelphia, Pennsylvania, below. He listened to the clip-clop sound of horses' hooves and the clatter of carriage wheels rolling on the street. He watched the people of the city. He knew that his friends, John Adams and Ben Franklin, were somewhere nearby. They were probably worrying about how he was doing with the job before him. But they would not bother him. They knew he needed to be alone.

Jefferson returned to his desk. He picked up the pen and dipped it into the ink. When he finished, he held one of the most important documents ever written, the Declaration of Independence. Its call for freedom and human rights would ring like a bell of liberty throughout the world and change the course of history.

SON OF A PLANTER

Thomas Jefferson was born on April 13, 1743. His mother, Jane, was from the important Randolph family of Virginia. His father, Peter, had built a large tobacco plantation, or farm, in Virginia, near the Blue Ridge Mountains. He called the plantation Shadwell after the town in Britain where Jane's mother had been born. With the help of slave labor, Peter Jefferson became wealthy growing tobacco in America. The crop was stored in sturdy barrels, called hogsheads.

IT'S A FACT!

Peter Jefferson married William Randolph's sister Jane.

It was shipped by wagon or boat down the narrow Rivanna River to the James River. There it was loaded onto large ships and sent across the Atlantic Ocean to Britain.

Peter Jefferson was admired in Virginia as an explorer and surveyor. He braved the dangers of the American wilderness to map out large areas of land. Peter helped draw the first complete map of Virginia. On one surveying trip, he and his group were attacked by wild animals. At night, they had to sleep in the trees to keep safe. Peter was also famous for his strength. Some people said that he could lift two hogsheads of tobacco, weighing one thousand pounds each.

At the time Thomas Jefferson was born, Virginia was one of thirteen American colonies ruled by Great Britain. Peter Jefferson was a member of the Virginia House of Burgesses. This

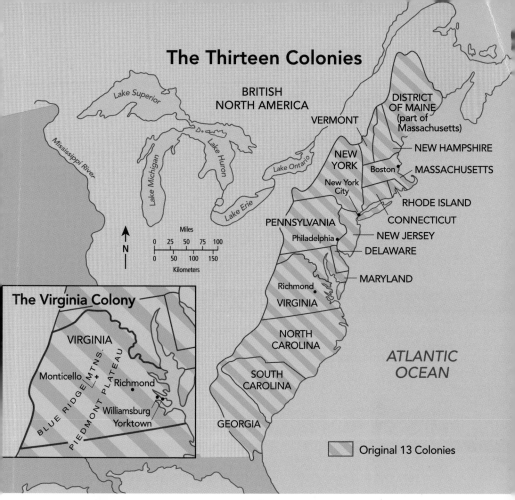

The Thirteen Colonies

BRITISH
NORTH AMERICA

Lake Superior

VERMONT

DISTRICT
OF MAINE
(part of
Massachusetts)

NEW HAMPSHIRE

Mississippi River

Lake Michigan

Lake Huron

Lake Ontario

Lake Erie

NEW
YORK

Boston

MASSACHUSETTS

New York
City

RHODE ISLAND

PENNSYLVANIA

CONNECTICUT

Philadelphia

NEW JERSEY

DELAWARE

Miles

0 25 50 75 100

N

0   50   100 150

Kilometers

MARYLAND

Richmond

VIRGINIA

The Virginia Colony

VIRGINIA

Monticello

BLUE RIDGE MTNS.

Richmond

PIEDMONT PLATEAU

Williamsburg

Yorktown

NORTH
CAROLINA

SOUTH
CAROLINA

GEORGIA

ATLANTIC
OCEAN

Original 13 Colonies

**The thirteen American colonies were under British rule
when Thomas Jefferson was born in 1743.**

group made laws for the colony, which was
governed by the British royal governor. Peter was a
colonel of the militia, a group of part-time
volunteer soldiers. His job was to keep order on the
frontier. He did this by becoming friends with
Native Americans from the area. He often invited
them to his house.

In 1745, when Tom was two years old, his
uncle William Randolph died. Before Randolph's
death, Peter had agreed to take care of his
plantation and his three children. The Jefferson
family moved from Shadwell to the larger
Randolph plantation, called Tuckahoe.

GROWING UP IN VIRGINIA

Tom always remembered how a servant carried him
on horseback on top of a pillow on the way to
Tuckahoe. His new home was much nicer than
Shadwell. The Jefferson
children played with the
young Randolphs. Tutors
came to the home to teach
the children. Tom even
took dancing lessons. The
family stayed at Tuckahoe
for seven years. When the
Randolph children were old enough to be on their
own, the Jefferson family returned home to
Shadwell.

IT'S A FACT!
By the time he was
six, Tom had read
most of the books in
his father's library.

Tom was nine when he returned to Shadwell.
Even though the plantation was huge and far from
any cities, Tom never felt lonely. The Jefferson

family was large. Tom had two older sisters, Jane and Mary, and three younger ones, Elizabeth, Martha, and Lucy. Later, the twins, Anna and Randolph, were born.

Peter Jefferson gave a lot of attention to his first-born son. Young Tom dreamed of becoming a surveyor and explorer just like his father. Tom's parents wanted him to have a good education. Few schools were available. So boys like Tom often were sent to stay with an educated man. The man would be his tutor.

Peter also wanted his son to be strong physically and mentally. He taught him to love outdoor sports. Young Tom hunted, fished, swam, and rode horseback. Peter also made sure that Tom knew how to run a plantation. He learned how to make a round barrel out of pieces of wood. He could churn cream into butter. He also knew how to separate healthy tobacco leaves from unhealthy ones.

IT'S A FACT!

Tom wasn't a good hunter. When he was ten years old, his father gave him a rifle and sent him out to hunt. The only thing Tom shot was a wild turkey that had already been caught in a pen.

At about this time, he was sent to study and live with the Reverend William Douglas in Northam, fifty miles from home. Tom's father gave him a Latin dictionary as a going-away gift. Tom did not like Douglas. He was tough. Tom liked Mrs. Douglas's cooking even less. He studied hard, learning Greek, Latin, and French. He even memorized the rules of manners that gentlemen of the time had to know. These rules included "Spit not, cough not, nor blow thy nose at table."

During Tom's five years at school, he always looked forward to coming home. He spent the long summers at Shadwell. He enjoyed spending time

Tom spent much of his childhood at Shadwell. He enjoyed wandering across its huge fields.

with his favorite sister, Jane. They explored the hillsides on foot. During their walks, they often looked at a beautiful mountaintop about a mile away. Tom thought that he'd like to live on the mountain someday. His summer vacations also gave him time to hunt and fish with his friends.

When Tom was fourteen, his happy life changed forever. In the summer of 1757, his father became ill. The doctors didn't know how to cure him. Peter's health quickly got worse. He died on August 17. His dying words to his wife were about Tom. He wanted her to be sure Tom's education continued. He also wanted to leave Tom his surveying tools, his cherrywood writing desk, and his library of forty books.

Peter Jefferson had been Tom's hero. His goal in life was to be just like his father. The boy had dreamed of exploring the wilderness at Peter's side. But now his father was gone and that could never happen. Tom was crushed. He missed his father desperately.

2

THE SCHOLAR

TOM NEVER FORGOT how he felt after his father's death. It was an event that changed his life. Suddenly, as the oldest son, he was responsible for his whole family. His mother, six sisters, and one brother needed him to take charge. His father's will split the estate between Tom and his brother, Randolph. Tom inherited the property containing the house where he had been born. Tom's mother and sisters were also provided for. Mrs. Jefferson was given the use of the house and farm for the rest of her life.

Peter had known that his children would not legally get their inheritance until the age of twenty-one. So he had asked five men to help the family until then. These guardians allowed Tom to continue his education. The first decision he made on his own was to change schools. He didn't think Douglas offered him a good enough education. Tom went to study with the Reverend Dr. Joseph Maury, only fourteen miles from Shadwell.

STUDYING WITH DR. MAURY

Dr. Maury taught Tom Latin, Greek, French, and Italian. He had a library of four hundred books. Tom spent many hours reading the books and taking notes. Dr. Maury gave Tom violin lessons. He practiced the violin three hours a day. He also made friends with other students, including Dabney Carr. Carr remained Tom's closest friend all through school, college, and beyond.

One of the best things about Dr. Maury's school was its closeness to Shadwell. Tom was able to go home on weekends. Often Carr

Tom liked to play his violin. It looked like this one.

IT'S A FACT!

Tom was tall for his age. His friends at school called him Tall Tom.

came with him. They studied together. They hiked through the woods and fields to a hill called Little Mountain. There, Tom and Dabney made a deal. They promised that if one died, the other would bury him beneath the spreading oak tree where they stood.

Tom and his sister Jane grew even closer. They enjoyed walking and talking together. They both loved music. Jane often sang while Tom played his violin.

After two years, Dr. Maury agreed that Tom was ready for college. First, Tom had to convince his guardians. He wrote them a letter telling them that he wanted to go to the College of William and Mary in Williamsburg, Virginia. "By going to college," he wrote, "I shall get a more universal acquaintance which may ... be serviceable to me. I can pursue my studies in Greek and Latin ... and likewise learn something of Mathematics."

The guardians agreed. In the spring of 1760, Tom rode on horseback to Williamsburg. He was almost seventeen years old.

COLLEGE YEARS

Williamsburg was the capital of Virginia. It was a small, beautiful city with a main street more than one mile long. At one end was the capitol building. The College of William and Mary stood at the other end of the main street.

Tom settled into college life easily. He often spent time at the Raleigh Tavern. He also went dancing at a ballroom called the Apollo Room. Although he was a bit shy, he was popular. He was charming and easy to get along with. He was an excellent conversationalist and had good manners. He quickly became a favorite

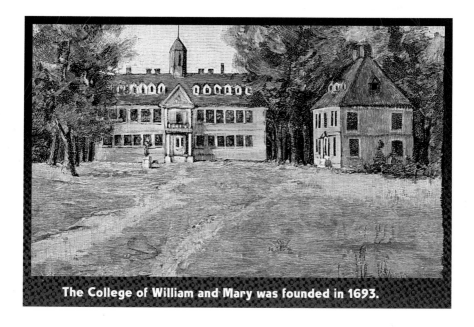

The College of William and Mary was founded in 1693.

among his fellow students. He was also popular with the young women of the town.

Tom became friends with a professor of mathematics, Dr. William Small. Small was more than just a mathematician. He was a deep thinker and a philosopher. He introduced his students to exciting new ideas. He taught them to use reason in their thinking. In his memoirs, Thomas Jefferson describes Small as "a man profound in . . . science with . . . an enlarged and liberal mind . . . [who] made me his daily companion." He went on to write that knowing Dr. Small "probably fixed the destinies of my life."

Small taught Tom about the new scientific method. This way of thinking uses observations and experiments to come to accurate conclusions. Tom was fascinated. He was eager to use this method in practical ways. On vacations at Shadwell, he figured out a better way to rotate the crops. By planting different crops in the fields each year, a farmer could keep the soil fresh and rich. Rich soil tends to grow better and stronger crops.

GAINING MORE KNOWLEDGE

William Small saw that the young, tall, red-headed Tom had unusual ability. He introduced Tom to two

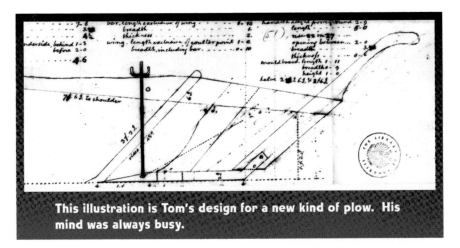

This illustration is Tom's design for a new kind of plow. His mind was always busy.

other men who had an impact on the young man. One was George Wythe, a lawyer. Jefferson called Wythe a "faithful and beloved mentor in youth . . . and my most affectionate friend through life." He added that Wythe was "devoted . . . to liberty and the natural and equal rights of man." The other man was the royal governor of Virginia, Francis Fauquier. According to Jefferson, Fauquier was "the ablest man ever to hold that office."

This group of four men spent many hours together. The older men saw something in Tom that interested them. Tom was

George Wythe

glad to have the chance to learn all he could from the educated and worldly men. The talks he shared with them contained "more good sense, more rational and philosophical conversation than in all my life," he wrote. These friends set Tom upon the course he would follow in life. "In a moment of temptation or difficulty," he wrote, "I would ask myself, 'What would Dr. Small, Mr. Wythe . . . do in this situation[?]' "

IT'S A FACT!

Although Tom was a good student, he often left his homework until the last minute. He often locked himself in his room to finish the assigned work.

Tom always wanted to learn more. He studied math, physics, natural science, astronomy, agriculture, history, and languages. He often studied fifteen hours a day, reading past midnight. Then he got up early in the morning to start again.

NEW FRIENDS

Tom also found time to enjoy friends his own age. His boyhood friend Dabney Carr studied at William and Mary too. Tom also became friends with John Tyler, another hardworking student, and with Patrick

Henry, who was studying law. And Tom continued
to be a favorite with the young women.

While at college, Tom
fell in love for the first
time. The young woman's
name was Rebecca Burwell.
She was pretty and
popular. Tom wrote about
his feelings for Rebecca in
letters and poems that he
never sent to her. But
Rebecca married someone
else. Tom's first romance
was over before it had really begun.

IT'S A FACT!
Tom met Patrick
Henry in 1759 at a
Christmas party.
Both of them played
the violin and
performed for the
other guests long
into the night.

The college years flew by. In 1762, Tom finished
his studies at William and Mary. At nineteen, he had
to make a decision. He could go home and live the
life of a gentleman planter. Tom loved Shadwell. But
he made another choice. He wanted to try to
accomplish something greater in the world.

3

THE YOUNG LAWYER

THOMAS JEFFERSON GRADUATED from the College of William and Mary in 1762. He could speak Greek, Latin, French, and Italian. He had read the works of ancient and modern philosophers. He had studied science and math. Nineteen-year-old Jefferson was one of the best-educated men in Virginia.

STUDYING LAW WITH WYTHE

Jefferson's friends–Dabney Carr, John Tyler, and Patrick Henry–had decided to study law. Jefferson liked the idea as well. At that time, the colonies had no law schools. A young man

became a lawyer by studying with an attorney.
Virginia lawyer George Wythe happily agreed to
take on his young friend as an apprentice (student).
Many people thought
Wythe was the best
teacher of law in Virginia.
Many of Wythe's students
later became leaders. His
favorite was always Tom
Jefferson.

IT'S A FACT!
When Wythe died
years later, the old
lawyer left all his
books to Jefferson.

Jefferson learned from
the older man's experience and knowledge of the
law. Jefferson wanted to know everything. He
believed he could understand the laws of his day
by studying those of the past. He read about legal
history back to ancient Roman and Greek times.
Jefferson even learned to read old English laws in
their original form. He wrote everything in a
notebook that he called his Commonplace Book.
This was one of many notebooks that Jefferson
kept. He used the notebooks to keep track of
everything in his life.

Jefferson had to stay in Williamsburg in order
to study with Wythe. While there, he shared rooms
with fellow law student John Tyler. In addition to

his law studies, Jefferson observed the stars and recorded weather activity. He practiced the violin daily. With his friends, he went to dances, dinners, and the theater. As part of his legal training, he attended court sessions. He made notes about everything he saw.

This page is from one of Jefferson's legal notebooks.

Jefferson studied with Wythe for five years. During that time, he turned twenty-one and took over the management of Shadwell. He returned home often to check on the plantation. Jefferson loved his home and tried to improve it. On his twenty-first birthday in 1764, he planted an avenue of locust trees there. He also thought about his dream of building a house at the top of Little Mountain. He taught himself about architecture (designing buildings) so he would one day be able to design his perfect home.

Dabney Carr was also studying law. He went to Shadwell with Jefferson. They enjoyed exploring the area's hills and valleys. They paddled canoes across the river. They spent hours discussing law, philosophy, and literature.

During these visits to Shadwell, Carr grew to know the Jefferson family well. He liked them all. But soon, his feelings for Jefferson's younger sister Martha grew deeper. The couple fell in love and were married at Shadwell in July 1765. Jefferson's best friend was now a part of his family. In a letter a few years later, Jefferson described Carr after his marriage. "In a very small house, with a table, half a dozen chairs . . . the happiest man in the universe."

A Painful Loss

Jefferson returned to Williamsburg after the wedding. A week later, his joy turned to sadness. A message told him that his beloved older sister Jane had become ill and died. She was twenty-five years old. The news crushed him. He had felt closer to Jane than to anyone else in his family.

Jane had always loved flowers. Soon after her death, Jefferson began to plant and raise flowers. He kept a "Garden Book" where he made notes about them. In this journal, he kept a record of the flowering and death of every blossom in his garden.

Jefferson returned to Williamsburg and his law books. He finished his studies and became a lawyer. People suggested

IT'S A FACT!

Jefferson never got over the loss of his beloved sister. When he was planning his hilltop home, he built a family cemetery and had Jane's body moved there. He tried to make the spot as beautiful as possible for her. Jefferson's grandchildren said that, even in old age, he still spoke about Jane "in terms of as warm admiration and love as if the grave had but just closed over her."

that he start his practice in Williamsburg. But
Jefferson wanted to live on his farm. "Those who
labour in the earth," he wrote, "are the chosen
people of God."

He returned to his plans for his house on Little
Mountain. He read books on Italian architecture.
Soon he began to draw plans for a classic home
with beautiful gardens and orchards.

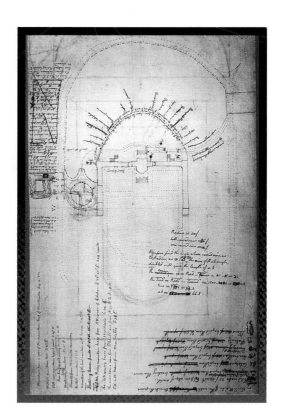

**This drawing shows
Jefferson's plans
for the garden of
his new house.**

Jefferson called the new house Monticello. The word means "little mountain" in Italian.

Monticello was only four miles from Shadwell. Jefferson needed to be near his family. He was responsible for his mother and the four children still at home.

MOVING TOWARD REVOLUTION

For all of Jefferson's life to this point, the thirteen American colonies belonged to Britain. Americans thought of themselves as British citizens. They were loyal subjects of the British king, George III. Most were proud to be part of the powerful British Empire. But as time passed, differences appeared between the colonists and Great Britain. Many colonists began to think about independence.

In the mid-1760s, the British Parliament (government) passed the Stamp Act. This law was to help Britain pay for a war it had fought earlier. The Stamp Act said that colonists had to pay a tax on every document they used, including newspapers and letters. The colonists were angry about the tax. They were not allowed to vote to elect Parliament members. So they saw the new law as "taxation without representation." The colonists asked King

Colonists rally to oppose the Stamp Act.

George to get rid of the tax. But the king refused. In Virginia, Thomas Jefferson's friend Patrick Henry made a speech saying that only elected representatives of the people had the right to make laws.

After Patrick Henry's speech, Americans grew even angrier. Many colonists rioted and refused to pay the hated tax. Two years later, Parliament finally got rid of the Stamp Act. The colonists were very happy, but King George and Parliament were angry.

Not long afterward, Parliament passed the Townshend Act. It required the colonists to pay a tax on almost every item shipped from Britain. Most goods in the colonies came from the British Empire. The colonists were angry. Soon violent protests began again. The seeds were slowly being sown for rebellion.

THE TRAVELING LAWYER

Despite the political distractions, Jefferson focused on taking care of his family. To do this, he needed to make money through his law practice. He handled dozens of cases every year. He quickly became a respected attorney and built one of the largest legal practices in Virginia. He rode about two hundred miles a month visiting clients and courts around the colony.

In 1768, when he was twenty-five, Jefferson was elected to the Virginia House of Burgesses. He was proud to be following in the footsteps of his father. From the start, Jefferson took a stand against slavery. Slave owners in Virginia were not allowed to set their own slaves free. One of Jefferson's first actions in the House of Burgesses was to propose a law that would allow them to do so. His law did not pass.

THE HOWELL CASE

One of Jefferson's best-known legal cases involved a slave named Samuel Howell. At the time, slavery was legal and common in Virginia. Howell claimed he had the right to freedom because his great-grandmother had been a free white woman. Jefferson knew that Howell was sure to lose his case. He also knew that the slave could not pay him. But he took the case because he felt it was the right thing to do. He argued that under the law of nature, all people are born free. The judge was shocked and angry. He ruled against Howell. But the case had given Jefferson his first chance to share his ideas about freedom and liberty.

Jefferson was sure that slavery was a sin. Yet his own plantation was run by slaves. In his heart, he knew slavery was wrong. He worked to end it by law. But he never freed his own slaves.

The other burgesses quickly discovered Jefferson's best talents. Jefferson was not a great speaker. But he was a great writer. He could write clearly and knew how to use words well. He was often asked to write out new laws and other papers.

CHAPTER 4
TRAGEDIES AND JOYS

IN FEBRUARY 1770, Jefferson got shocking news. A fire at Shadwell had burned his childhood home almost to the ground. The servant who brought the news said that the family was safe. Jefferson's violin had been rescued. But all the books he had spent his life collecting had burned. "Would to God it had been money," he wrote to a friend. "Then it never would have cost me a sigh." For Jefferson, books were more valuable than gold.

STARTING MONTICELLO

Jefferson also continued to work on Monticello, his
dream home. He didn't hire an architect to create
the plans for his home. He studied buildings of the
past and present and learned more about
architecture. He drew up his own plans for the
house and gardens. He even drew details for the
other buildings that were needed on a plantation.
These included kitchens, stables, and the
smokehouse for preserving foods.

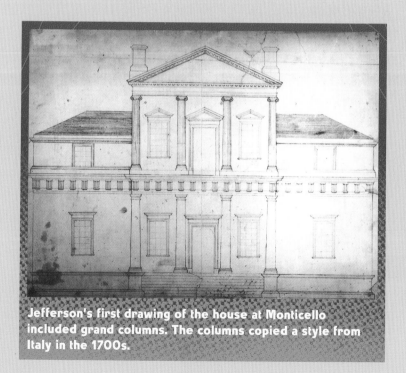

Jefferson's first drawing of the house at Monticello
included grand columns. The columns copied a style from
Italy in the 1700s.

IT'S A FACT!

A skilled gardener named Bernard McMahon influenced Jefferson's Monticello gardens. McMahon had written *The American Gardener's Calendar*. Jefferson trusted McMahon's views. McMahon, in return, sent Jefferson unusual plants, such as Egyptian onion and sugarloaf cabbage.

It was the main house, however, on which Jefferson spent the most time. He constantly made changes. He wanted a house and gardens different from any other in America. He wanted it to have beauty and grace. At the same time, it had to be a comfortable home. Monticello was to be a reflection of Thomas Jefferson.

Soon after the fire at Shadwell, workers completed a small brick building on Monticello. It was a tiny space, but Jefferson was so eager to be living at Monticello that he moved in.

LOVE AND MARRIAGE

During this time, Jefferson met a twenty-one-year-old widow named Martha Wayles Skelton. Martha was the daughter of his friend and fellow attorney John Wayles. He described Martha as "a most agreeable companion, full of pleasantry and good humor." Martha had married young. But her husband had died soon after their marriage. When Jefferson met her, she had a three-year-old son. Jefferson loved the boy, but he grew ill and died before he turned four.

Martha was beautiful, tall, and slim. She was educated and could talk about books and current events. She also loved music. Just as he had with his sister Jane, Jefferson played his violin while Martha sang. Sometimes she played a pianolike instrument called a harpsichord. Other times, they just sang together.

The couple spent more and more time together. Jefferson often visited her at The Forest, her father's home. On January 1, 1772, Thomas and Martha were married there. It was a happy

IT'S A FACT!

The violin was fairly common among wealthy colonists. This was partly because pianos, another favorite, were expensive to ship from Britain to the colonies. Despite the expense, Jefferson bought Martha a piano as her wedding present.

event with music played by fiddlers. Jefferson was twenty-eight and Martha was twenty-three. They set off on the hundred-mile trip to begin their life together at Monticello.

On the way, they ran into a bad snowstorm. It was the worst storm in many years. Soon two feet of snow covered the narrow roads. They had to leave their coach behind and continue on horseback. Swirling snow swept over them. They shivered in the cold wind. Finally, they arrived at Monticello. The couple had to find their way in the dark to the little brick building, where they lived while the main house was being completed. All the fires had gone out. The servants were asleep in their own houses. The building had just one room. The small space, Jefferson wrote, served for "parlor, for kitchen and hall . . . for bedchamber and study, too."

This could have been an unpleasant beginning to a marriage. Instead, the young couple treated it as an adventure. They laughed and joked as they lit candles. The room was filled with books and furniture. They had wine and music and each other. Later, Jefferson described to a friend how he and Martha

Jefferson and Martha spent their first winter together in this small cabin.

"refreshed themselves . . . and startled the silence of the night with song and merry laughter."

Not long after the marriage, Martha's father died. Martha's inheritance almost doubled the size of the couple's property. She also inherited

HUNTINGTON CITY-TOWNSHIP
PUBLIC LIBRARY
200 W. Market Street
Huntington IN 46750

THE HEMINGS FAMILY

When John Wayles, Jefferson's father-in-law, died in 1773, Jefferson inherited all of Wayles's slaves. They included the Hemings family. Betty Hemings was John Wayles's mistress, and her children were Martha Jefferson's half brothers and half sisters. As a result, Jefferson made sure that very little work was required of the family. He also made sure that the Hemings boys were taught a trade.

many slaves. Jefferson still opposed slavery. But now he owned even more slaves than before.

NEW JOYS AND STRUGGLES

On September 27, 1772, Martha gave birth to a daughter. They named the girl Martha but called her Patsy. Patsy was sick at first. For months, her parents worried whether she would survive. But Patsy grew strong and healthy. (A second daughter, Jane Randolph, was born on April 3, 1774.)

Jefferson's life was busier than ever. He had to keep track of even more farmland. He also had to supervise the building of Monticello. His law practice brought him as many cases as he could handle.

Jefferson and Martha enjoyed their time
together and with friends. They often saw Dabney
Carr and his family. Carr was also a successful
lawyer. Like Jefferson, he was a member of the
House of Burgesses. Unlike Jefferson, he was an
exciting speaker. After his first speech, people
predicted that he would have a bright future.
Jefferson was happy about his friend's success.

Soon after that first speech, Dabney Carr
grew ill. An infection quickly spread through his
body. He died on May 16, 1773. Jefferson was
away at the time. As soon as he heard the news,
he hurried home to discover that his friend had
already been buried at Shadwell. Jefferson had not
forgotten the promise he and Carr had made so
many years before. He moved his friend's body to
a spot near the old oak tree on Monticello where
they had spent so many hours. On Carr's
gravestone, Jefferson had inscribed: "To his Virtue,
Good Sense, Learning, and Friendship this stone is
dedicated by Thomas Jefferson, who of all men
living, loved him most."

Martha Carr had loved her husband deeply.
His early death was very hard on her and their six
young children. Jefferson promised his sister that

he would always take care of her and the children. Soon he took them into his home.

Jefferson's life was full of responsibility. But outside events were happening that would soon sweep him into a world of ideas and action.

CHAPTER 5
REVOLUTION AND A NEW NATION

VIRGINIA'S GOVERNOR at this time was loyal to Britain. When protests against British laws reached Virginia, he shut down the House of Burgesses. Twenty-eight burgesses continued to meet at the Raleigh Tavern in Williamsburg. Jefferson was among them. So were George Washington and Patrick Henry.

They agreed to boycott, or stop buying, British goods. They would have to do without new clothing, spices, tea, paint, and jewelry. Jefferson worked hard to organize people for the boycott in his own county of Albemarle. Late that year, Virginia's governor called for new elections for the House of Burgesses. Almost all the old members were reelected.

(Above) American colonists meet to talk about how unhappy they are under British rule.

British merchants were hurt by these boycotts. They asked Parliament to cancel the taxes. The only one left in place was a tax on tea. By this time, the idea of American freedom from British rule was spreading. Jefferson had wondered what it would be like to be free of Great Britain. Everything he had learned convinced him that King George's actions were unfair and illegal.

PROTESTS GROW IN THE COLONIES

In 1773, a group of people in Boston protested the tax on tea. Dressed as Native Americans, they boarded a ship in Boston Harbor and tossed the tea overboard. This event, which became known as the Boston Tea Party, angered King George. The British closed Boston Harbor and sent troops of red-coated British soldiers to control the city. Virginians

IT'S A FACT!

The men who tossed out the tea were members of the Sons of Liberty. This secret organization used mob attacks to show their dislike of British rule. A Boston businessman named Samuel Adams was one of the group's leaders.

The Sons of Liberty dressed as Native Americans for the Boston Tea Party in 1773.

supported the protesters. Lord Dunmore, the new governor of Virginia, closed the House of Burgesses again.

Still, the Burgesses continued to meet. In 1774, Jefferson wrote out the group's thoughts in a series of essays called *A Summary View of the Rights of British America*. He argued that the first colonists had been free in Britain before they came to the colonies. In America, they were still free people. But they had no representatives in the British Parliament. Because of this, he said that Parliament had no right to make laws for the colonies. He begged King George to cooperate with the colonists for peace. The *Summary View* was published and read throughout the colonies. Jefferson's words caught the public's imagination. They liked his ideas about choosing their own government.

These ideas might have faded if Britain had
listened to the colonists' demands. Instead, the king
sent more British troops to America. In the fall of
1774, colonial leaders called for a Continental
Congress to meet in Philadelphia. Representatives
came from all of the colonies except Georgia.
Jefferson was ill, so he was unable to attend the
Congress. But Patrick Henry was there. The Congress
decided that the colonies must stand together. After
the Congress, Virginia leaders met in Richmond,
Virginia, to support that idea. Thomas Jefferson was
at this meeting.

IT'S A FACT!

Patrick Henry *(far
right)* was at the
Congress meeting in
Richmond. He
declared, "Is life so
dear or peace so
sweet as to be
purchased at the
price of chains
and slavery? . . .
Give me liberty or
give me death!"

In April 1775, farmers in Massachusetts formed militias to protect themselves from the British soldiers. Bloody battles were fought at Lexington and Concord between the militias and the British soldiers. The American Revolution had begun.

SUMMER SESSION

Jefferson was elected as a delegate (representative) from Virginia to the Second Continental Congress in Philadelphia. The meeting was held in the summer of 1775. Already, colonists were fighting British troops, especially in and around Boston. Some delegates still hoped they could come to an agreement with King George. They wrote a letter to him. He refused to read it. Most colonial leaders realized that the king would never grant the colonies their freedom. The Congress began to prepare for war with Great Britain. The delegates spent the hot and sticky summer debating inside Carpenters' Hall (later called Independence Hall).

Thomas Jefferson rarely spoke on the main floor. He was more comfortable speaking in front of small groups. But the group did know that he was an excellent writer. They asked him to do much of the writing for the Congress.

Most of Jefferson's ideas agreed with those of
John Adams from Massachusetts. Like Jefferson,
Adams was a scholar and a writer. Like Jefferson, he
believed that the colonies should be independent.
But Jefferson and Adams were also opposites in
many ways. Jefferson was a southern gentleman.
Adams was a northern farmer. Jefferson was tall
and lean. Adams was short and stout. Adams was
outgoing and talkative. Jefferson was shy and quiet.
Despite these differences, they became good
friends. They shared a love of learning. They both
believed that whatever happened in Philadelphia
would be very important. Adams wrote about his
new friend, "He was so prompt, frank . . . and
decisive upon committees and in conversation . . .
that he soon seized my heart."

Jefferson also met Benjamin Franklin of
Pennsylvania. Franklin, the oldest member of the
Congress, had gray hair and a wrinkled face. But
his eyes sparkled with wisdom. Franklin was famous
around the world as a printer, inventor, writer, and
scientist.

Soon after Jefferson's arrival in Philadelphia,
George Washington was named commander in chief
of the Continental Army. The colonists were not

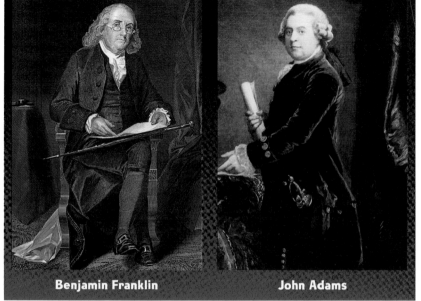

Benjamin Franklin   John Adams

trained for battle. General Washington's job was to organize volunteers, mostly farmers, into a real fighting force. The Americans were determined to resist the British, but they were untrained for battle. But the men believed in Washington.

Jefferson worked hard as debates continued into the fall. But his heart was at Monticello. He worried about the crops. He always thought about his daughters and wife. Martha was often ill. In September 1775, he rode home for a short visit to find that another tragedy had struck the family. His

baby daughter Jane had died. Martha's grief made
her poor health even worse. Jefferson hated leaving
her at such a time. But he had to go back to
Philadelphia.

Jefferson's work for the Congress was
important, but being separated from his family was
becoming harder and harder. He wrote letters home
regularly but heard nothing in return for almost

Jefferson's
wife, Martha,
was often ill.

two months. "The suspense under which I am is too terrible to be endured," he wrote in a letter to his brother-in-law. "If anything has happened, for god's sake, let me know it."

Finally, Jefferson received a letter from Martha saying that all was well. Still, he feared for the health and safety of his family. The fighting had spread to Virginia. The British military now ruled the area. British soldiers burned down the city of Norfolk, Virginia. The governor offered rewards to those who would side with the British. He offered to free slaves who joined his army. Jefferson had to go home. In December, although Congress was still meeting, he left for Monticello.

Jefferson remained at Monticello for four months. Martha needed him. She was heartbroken over Jane's death. Jefferson also had to care for his mother, who was seriously ill. She died on March 31, 1776, at the age of fifty-seven. Jefferson mourned his mother deeply. For weeks, he suffered terrible headaches. They sometimes lasted entire days. He described them as "paroxysms [sudden attacks] of the most excruciating pain."

Despite his suffering, Jefferson continued to work for American freedom. He was elected to the

Committee of Safety in Albemarle County. This
group helped direct the local militia. He collected a
supply of gunpowder for the Virginia militia. He
also raised money to be sent to Boston, where food
and other supplies were needed.

Early in 1776, Jefferson read a pamphlet that
thrilled him. It was called *Common Sense* and was
written by Thomas Paine, who had recently come to
America from Britain. Paine called upon Americans
to create a democratic nation. *Common Sense* inspired
the colonists. But Jefferson was getting ready to
write an even more important document.

DECLARATION OF INDEPENDENCE

Jefferson, aged thirty-three, returned to Philadelphia
in May 1776. He was chosen for a committee that
would write a declaration, explaining why the
colonies were separating from Great Britain. Other
leaders on the committee included Benjamin
Franklin and John Adams. They agreed that
Jefferson should write this important declaration.
"You can write ten times better than I can," Adams
told him.

Jefferson went to the rooms he had rented on
the second floor of a house in Philadelphia. He

dipped his pen into the ink and began to write. As he wrote the Declaration of Independence, he thought about all that had happened in recent years. "We hold these truths to be self-evident," he wrote, "that all men are created equal, that they are endowed by their Creator with certain unalienable [firm] Rights, that among these are Life, Liberty, and the pursuit of Happiness."

IT'S A FACT!

Jefferson's first draft of the Declaration had included a call for an end to the slave trade. But this part was taken out of the final version. Jefferson knew it wasn't the time to argue. All of the colonies needed to be united. The southern states would never agree to outlaw slavery.

The delegates signed the Declaration on July 4, 1776. Each man knew that if the colonists failed, they would lose all they had. They might even be hanged. With their signatures, they promised to each other, "our Lives, our Fortunes, and our sacred Honor."

Copies of the Declaration were carried all over the colonies. In large cities and small villages, citizens gathered to hear it read. Bells rang out and

people cheered. A new nation–the United States of
America–was born.

But the fight for freedom was not going well.
Fourteen thousand people had fled Boston when
the British took over the city. General Washington
had rushed the Continental Army to nearby
Cambridge, Massachusetts. There, he received a
hero's welcome. John Adams's wife, Abigail,
described him as having "dignity with ease." Soon
the British left Boston and headed to New York.
Washington marched his untrained troops south to
meet the attack.

General William Howe led British forces to
victory in New York. Washington's army lost many
men and was forced to retreat. The British followed
the shattered Continental forces across New Jersey.
In December 1776, those who were left rowed
across the Delaware River to Pennsylvania. Things
looked bad for the Americans.

Their hopes rose when Washington took his
troops back across the Delaware on Christmas Eve
for a surprise attack. But there were many more
defeats than victories during the next few years.
One of the lowest points for the Americans came
during the winter of 1777. Soldiers froze and

Many American soldiers died in the camp at Valley Forge.

starved at their winter camp at Valley Forge, Pennsylvania.

In the early years of the American Revolution, not much of the fighting was in Virginia. During that time, Thomas Jefferson stayed at Monticello with his family. "Peach trees and cherry trees at Monticello begin to blossom," he wrote in his notebook. He continued work on the house and kept reading. In May 1777, Martha gave birth to a son, but the baby died. A year later, the Jeffersons had a healthy baby daughter. They named her Mary, nicknamed Polly.

NEW GOVERNMENT FOR VIRGINIA

Jefferson worked on the new government that was being set up in Virginia. He believed that the colonies would win independence. He wanted the new nation to have a government that would represent and protect the people. He hoped to take the first steps in Virginia. Jefferson felt that citizens of a democracy should be educated and able to support themselves. He wanted a public school system that would give every child a good education. He wanted to give small farms to people who owned no land. He wanted to end slavery. But the older lawmakers in Virginia voted down many of his ideas.

In Virginia, the government supported the Anglican Church (the Church of England). It was the official church of most people. They all had to pay taxes to pay for the church. But Jefferson believed that religion and government should be run separately. He wrote a new plan that said "all men shall be free to profess and maintain . . . their opinions in matter of religion." Virginia lawmakers agreed to Jefferson's plan for freedom of religion in Virginia. They made his plan a law. Jefferson considered it one of his most important achievements.

CHAPTER 6
THE WAR CONTINUES

IN 1779, Thomas Jefferson was elected governor of Virginia. He was thirty-six years old. Jefferson wanted Virginia to be a model for the new country. But trouble was coming. The British were attacking the state. The war took up most of Jefferson's time.

(Above) The British often set fire to farms and towns in Virginia.

THE WAR IN VIRGINIA

A British fleet (group of warships) attacked Virginia a month before Jefferson took office. Eighteen thousand British redcoats marched through the countryside. They destroyed crops and burned whole towns. Jefferson tried to get troops and supplies, but the state had little money. The Virginia militia wasn't well trained. It lacked arms and supplies.

53

In January 1781, the British took Richmond. The British troops set fire to the city. Virginia's government leaders had to move to Charlottesville, a city not far from Jefferson's home.

Jefferson wrote Congress to ask for help, but no help came. Personal problems added to Jefferson's troubles. In April 1780, Martha had given birth to their fifth child. The infant died in 1781, and Martha's health got worse. By June, the British were moving toward Charlottesville.

Jefferson rushed to Monticello. He sent his family to safety at another plantation. He stayed behind and went to nearby Carter's Mountain. There, he used a telescope to watch Charlottesville. At first, all was quiet. But soon, the streets had filled with British soldiers. Governor Jefferson ran to his horse and galloped off just in time. Ten minutes later, British troops took over Jefferson's home.

IT'S A FACT!

Jefferson's slaves had just hidden the family's silver in a secret place under the floor.

The house was empty except for two slaves. The British asked where Jefferson was. A soldier pointed a pistol at Martin, one of the slaves. He said he would shoot if Martin

During the American Revolution, British troops took over colonists' homes.

didn't tell him where Jefferson was. The slaves of Monticello were loyal to Jefferson. He had treated them kindly. "Fire away!" Martin told the soldier. The redcoat put down his pistol.

The British commander, Lord Banastre Tarleton, told his troops to leave Monticello as they had found it. No damage was done. Another British general acted differently. General Cornwallis's army captured a house at Elk Hill, another part of the Jefferson plantation. The British made it their headquarters. They stole anything they could use and destroyed everything else. They burned crops, fences, and barns. They killed the animals that were of no value to them. The slaves who lived at Elk Hill thought that the British would free them. Instead, the soldiers took the slaves and forced them to remain in the British camp. There, most of them died of smallpox or fever.

VICTORY FOR THE AMERICANS

By 1780, the war had started to turn in favor of the Americans. French troops and ships came to help in the fight. French ships blocked the British from reaching Virginia's coast along the Atlantic Ocean. A combined force of American and French troops fought the British army at Yorktown, Virginia. The British troops were outnumbered. On October 19, 1781, the British general surrendered. Small battles continued for another year, but the Americans had really won the war at Yorktown.

Shortly before the battle of Yorktown, Jefferson resigned as governor. At age thirty-eight, he was tired of politics. He felt he had given all he could give to his state and his country. Thomas Jefferson went home to Monticello. "I have retired to my farm, my family, and my books," he wrote to a friend, "from which I think nothing will ever more separate me."

This painting is by John Trumbull. It shows the surrender of British troops at Yorktown in 1781.

Soon after his return, Jefferson had an accident. He was thrown from his horse and was badly injured. He could not leave the house for many weeks.

A New Project

Despite his injuries, Jefferson kept busy. A Frenchman in Philadelphia named Francois de Barbe-Marbois wrote him a letter asking for information about Virginia. He asked twenty-one questions on many subjects. Answering these questions was a perfect project for Jefferson. He took up his pen and began to describe his state. He wrote about the state's rivers, cities, ports, boundaries, and

Jefferson put a lot of information about Virginia in his letters to the French diplomat Francois de Barbe-Marbois.

mountains. He described the forests, wildlife, trees, flowers, and fruit. He also wrote about the people and how they lived. He even mentioned the problems and evils of slavery. "I tremble for my country," he wrote, "when I reflect that God is just, that his justice cannot sleep forever."

Jefferson also wrote about Native Americans, whose culture had always interested him. He wrote about their history and languages. He discussed his dreams for his state and for the United States. Education and freedom of religion were among the most important of those dreams.

"Millions of innocent men, women and children, since the introduction of Christianity, have been burnt, tortured, fined, imprisoned," he wrote, "but it does me no injury for my neighbor to say there are twenty gods, or no god." Soon he had enough writing for a whole book. On December 20, 1781, he sent a copy of *Notes on the State of Virginia* to Barbe-Marbois. He called the work "very imperfect and not worth offering."

Notes on the State of Virginia contained many private thoughts. Jefferson never planned to publish them. He showed the writings only to a few close friends. They begged him to publish it. He refused, even when John Adams said, "The passages upon slavery are worth diamonds."

Four years later, Jefferson finally allowed two hundred copies to be printed in France. Even then, he took his name off the title page. Later, the book was printed in Britain and the United States.

The months that followed Jefferson's accident were among the happiest in his life. He worked on his book about Virginia. He gave his daughters, Patsy and Polly, extra attention. He also spent time with his sister's six children, who lived at Monticello with their mother. And he continued to supervise the building of Monticello.

IT'S A FACT!

By 1782, Jefferson owned more than four thousand acres of land and nearly two hundred slaves. Monticello included an eight-acre fruit garden.

Best of all, he spent most of his time with Martha. They worked together to run the house and plantation. They shared their love of music and conversation with each other and with a small group of good friends. Martha was pregnant again. But not all was well. Martha's health was still poor.

TRAGEDY STRIKES

In April 1782, Lucy Jefferson, their sixth child, was born. The birth left Martha ill and weak. Her health continued to get worse. Jefferson was very worried. He gave Martha all of his attention. For months, he insisted on caring for her himself. His daughter Patsy described her father during this time. "As a nurse, no female ever had more tenderness nor anxiety. He nursed my poor mother . . . sitting up with her and administering her medicines and drink to the last . . . he was never out of calling."

It was a hopeless struggle. On September 6, 1782, Martha died. Jefferson was heartbroken. "The violence of his emotion," his daughter wrote, "to this day I dare not describe to myself."

Jefferson shut himself up in his room and did not come out for three weeks. His family and friends worried for his health and safety. The

IT'S A FACT!

On her deathbed, Martha made Jefferson promise never to remarry. She didn't want her daughters to grow up with a stepmother, as she had. Jefferson agreed.

Thomas Jefferson who finally came out was a different man. His eyes were hollow, and his face was worn by sorrow. He tried to forget his grief through activity. "He was [always] on horseback," Patsy wrote, "rambling about the mountains . . . roads and . . . through the woods."

Jefferson wrote to a friend. "A single event wiped away all my plans and left me a blank, which I had not the spirit to fill in."

Jefferson had hoped to live out a peaceful life with Martha. That dream was gone. Thomas Jefferson, aged thirty-nine, never married again.

CHAPTER 7
BACK TO PUBLIC SERVICE

THOMAS JEFFERSON had three young daughters to care for. Patsy was ten, Polly was four, and Lucy was still a baby. Months passed after Martha's death, but Jefferson's grief did not lessen.

Jefferson admired the architecture he saw in Paris *(above)*.

FORMING THE NATION

Jefferson's friends were worried. Some of them decided that this might be a good time for him to return to public service. Congress asked him to be part of a team in Paris, France, that was working on a peace treaty (agreement) between

Great Britain and the United States. The fighting had ended between the two nations. But no official peace treaty had been signed. Other Americans, including Benjamin Franklin and John Adams, were already in Paris.

Jefferson had thought he would never leave Monticello again. But the main reason for him to stay was gone. He accepted the offer and traveled to Philadelphia in November 1782 to board a ship for Europe. The ship was unable to sail because it was stuck in thick ice. Jefferson stayed in Philadelphia for three months, waiting for the ice to melt. During that time, he met with old friends and again became interested in government.

Jefferson was still in Philadelphia when the treaty was signed in Paris. He no longer had a reason to go to France. In 1783, he was elected as a delegate to the U.S. Congress.

He left Monticello in November to join the new government. While serving in Congress, Jefferson often wrote to his children. He wrote that he loved them and told them to keep up with their educations.

In 1783, the United States was not a unified country. It was a loose group of thirteen states. The power of Congress was limited. This caused all sorts of problems. The new nation needed a stronger central government. Jefferson began to form plans for such a government. He thought of a new system of money using dollars, dimes, and pennies. He also had a plan for bringing new states into the country.

Once again, Congress asked Jefferson to go to France. This time, he was to join John Adams and Benjamin Franklin in working on trade agreements with France.

EARLY DAYS IN PARIS

On July 5, 1784, Jefferson and his daughter Patsy sailed out of Boston Harbor on a small ship called the *Ceres*. He left his younger daughters, Polly and Lucy, in the care of their mother's sister, Elizabeth Eppes. Jefferson had spent many hours reading about and studying the cultures of Europe. He was going to Paris, the cultural center of Europe at the time.

IT'S A FACT!

The Jefferson family owned a parrot named Shadwell. It went with Jefferson and Patsy on their trip to France.

Benjamin Franklin and John Adams were in Paris to greet Jefferson and Patsy. Franklin and Adams had already started work on an agreement that would allow the United States to trade freely with other nations. The Marquis de Lafayette, a French nobleman, also welcomed Jefferson to his country. They had become friends when Lafayette was in America fighting against the British. He introduced Jefferson to the most interesting and talented people in France.

Jefferson enjoyed Franklin's company. The two men shared many interests. Jefferson also spent time with his old friend John Adams and his wife, Abigail. Abigail called Jefferson "one of the choice ones of the world."

In Paris, Jefferson walked through the old streets. He admired the buildings, gardens, and art galleries. He made notes in his notebook about the details of the architecture he saw. He bought hundreds of books in the little bookstalls that lined the Seine River in Paris.

Jefferson also saw the problems with the city. A few wealthy people lived easy lives. Meanwhile, many men, women, and children were poor and hungry. Jefferson agreed with the ideas of freedom

and equality that were springing up all over
France. In fact, Jefferson's writings were read and
admired there.

THE NEW MINISTER TO FRANCE

Benjamin Franklin had represented the United
States in France for many years. He was seventy-
nine years old and in poor health. In 1785, he
returned home. Congress named Jefferson as the
new U.S. minister to France.

Jefferson knew that it would be a long time
before he would be able to go home. He wanted
his family together. Patsy was with him in France,
but Polly was still in Virginia with her aunt. Little
Lucy had died the year before at the age of two.
Lucy's death made Jefferson sure that he wanted to
have his family together in Paris. But Polly refused
to come. She liked her life and friends in Virginia.
Her father had to trick her into joining him. She
and some friends were sent to play aboard a ship
in the harbor. They enjoyed themselves and went
back time after time. One day, the children took
naps on the ship. The other girls were quietly
awakened and taken away. The ship then set sail
with the sleeping Polly aboard.

Polly was angry at first. But she soon began to enjoy the journey. In Paris, she finally saw her father and sister. They had been apart for four years. Soon Polly learned to enjoy life in Paris. She even called herself Maria, a French form of Mary, her real name.

Jefferson stayed in Europe for five years. He worked on trade agreements with the French. He traveled to other European countries. He drew or sent home examples of many objects new to him. Among these were a solar microscope and a thermometer. He also took note of new ideas, such as ways to improve crops. He even bought a copy machine called a Watt press.

Jefferson invented his own copying machine (left). He called it a polygraph. He used this machine to copy every letter he wrote. A polygraph uses two pens attached to each other. What one pen writes is automatically copied by the other pen.

MARIA COSWAY

When Maria Cosway met Jefferson, she was traveling with her husband, Richard Cosway, a well-known painter. Maria was sixteen years younger than Jefferson. She was short and thin and had a mass of curly blonde hair. She spoke six languages, played the harp and piano, and sang well. Jefferson was fascinated. For many weeks, she and Jefferson toured Paris and the French countryside. They began a flirtatious relationship.

During one of their outings, Jefferson badly broke his right wrist. The painful injury stopped their journeys. Maria didn't visit Jefferson or write to him. Eventually, she and her husband left France.

Her absence made Jefferson heartsick. He wrote her a twelve-page letter using his uninjured left hand. He called the letter a "Dialogue between Head and Heart." It was written as if it were a discussion between Jefferson's rational mind and his romantic heart. The letter begged Maria to reply with her own feelings. Her replies were friendly, not flirtatious. The relationship slowly ended.

Jefferson was often invited to the French king's court. He formed many new friendships, including one with Maria Cosway. Cosway was beautiful, talented, and popular in Paris. She and Jefferson spent hours together sharing their interest in music, art, and reading.

While Jefferson carried out his duties in France, a Constitutional Convention was meeting in Philadelphia to write the basic laws for the new

George Washington *(center, standing)* **leads a debate at the Constitutional Convention in 1787.**

American nation. Virginian James Madison wrote Jefferson often to tell him about the meetings. Jefferson wrote back with his own thoughts to Madison, Washington, and other friends. Even though Jefferson wasn't at the convention, many of his ideas were worked into the U.S. Constitution. Jefferson approved of most parts of the Constitution. But he was not satisfied until a Bill of Rights was added. The freedoms in the Bill of Rights, such as freedom of religion and trial by jury, were important to him.

Conditions in France were getting worse. Jefferson hoped that the French king and queen would make changes. But instead, they did nothing to help the suffering of their people. The winter of 1788–1789 was one of the coldest ever in Paris. People froze and starved on street corners. The French moved closer to revolution. Jefferson's friend Lafayette wrote a "Declaration of the Rights of Man." Jefferson's Declaration of Independence had inspired him. The king ignored Lafayette. In July 1789, the people of Paris stormed the Bastille jail. They let all of the prisoners go. The French Revolution (1789–1799) had begun.

On September 16, 1789, Jefferson's request to return home was approved. His job in Paris was over. Along with Patsy and Polly (now Maria), he got onto a ship to go home.

CHAPTER

8 NEW RESPONSIBILITIES

(Above) The gardens and farmland at Monticello kept Jefferson and his slaves busy.

IN 1789, JEFFERSON and his children sailed home to the United States on the *Clermont*. Near the U.S. coast, the ship ran into a storm and caught fire. It was a frightening trip. But the ship made it safely to port. Jefferson was home.

Jefferson had a lot of work to do at Monticello. The plantation had not been managed well while he was in France. Living

72

in France had been expensive. He was in debt (owed money) and needed time to get his life in order again. He hoped one day to return to France. But first, his country needed him.

In April 1789, George Washington had become the first president of the United States. Jefferson wrote to him from Paris. "There was nobody so well qualified as yourself," he wrote, "to put our new machine into a regular course of action."

Jefferson was home only a short time when he learned that Washington had picked him to be secretary of state. The secretary of state is one of a

George Washington was sworn in as the first president of the United States on April 30, 1789. The ceremony took place in New York City.

group of advisers to the president known as the cabinet. Jefferson's job would be to work with other countries. Jefferson wanted to stay at Monticello with his family. But the new job was important. He had to go. He prepared to go to New York City, which was the nation's capital at the time.

Members of George Washington's cabinet included (from left to right) Henry Knox, Thomas Jefferson, Alexander Hamilton, and Edmund Randolph.

A happy family event kept him at Monticello a while longer. Seventeen-year-old Patsy fell in love with her third cousin, Thomas Mann Randolph Jr. They wanted to marry. Jefferson liked Thomas Randolph. He was the son of Jefferson's cousin and close friend, Thomas Randolph Sr. Patsy and Randolph were married at Monticello on February 23, 1790. One week later, Jefferson left for his new job in New York.

DISAGREEMENTS WITH HAMILTON

Jefferson did not like working in an office. He got bad headaches while he worked. The headaches lasted all day. Still, Jefferson was working with people he knew and liked. He didn't expect any trouble. But soon, he began to have disagreements with Alexander Hamilton. Jefferson didn't believe that the central U.S. government should have too much power. Hamilton favored a strong central government.

The men first argued when Hamilton wanted the U.S. government to pay states' debts. Each of the states still owed money from the costs of fighting the American Revolution. Jefferson believed that paying the state's debts would give too much power to the central government. Most southerners agreed with Jefferson. The southern states had already paid a large part of their own debts. The men made a compromise. Hamilton agreed to eventually locate the nation's new capital in the South, in what would become Washington, D.C. In return, Jefferson and southern leaders went along with Hamilton's ideas about paying the states' debts.

This wasn't the only disagreement between the two men. Hamilton wanted to start a national bank to control the country's money. Jefferson disagreed. He felt a large central bank would

ALEXANDER HAMILTON

Alexander Hamilton and Jefferson strongly disagreed. But Hamilton still had the respect of early political leaders, including President George Washington. Hamilton thought the new United States should expand economically. He wanted to see balance between agriculture—Jefferson's way of making money—and manufacturing. Hamilton felt that merchants and other businesses would be important in the new country's future.

In 1801, the campaign for president was deadlocked. Both Jefferson and Aaron Burr, a man Hamilton strongly distrusted, had the same number of votes. According to the rules of the time, the U.S. Congress would choose between the two men. Hamilton supported Jefferson. Burr never forgave Hamilton. In 1804, the two men fought a duel. Hamilton died as a result of the fight.

ignore the needs of individuals and small
farmers. A national bank was not mentioned in
the Constitution. Jefferson argued that it would
be unconstitutional to have a national bank.
Hamilton said that the Constitution gave
Congress the power to make laws that were
necessary and proper. Jefferson lost this argument
when the Bank of the United States was created
in 1791.

One of the main duties of the secretary of
state is to help the president with foreign policy
(dealings with other nations). Jefferson and
Hamilton also disagreed on foreign policy. Great
Britain had refused to sign a trade agreement
with the United States. The British had also
broken the peace treaty that ended the American
Revolution by refusing to give up some of its
American forts. Jefferson wanted to take a strong
stand against the British by limiting trade with
them. But Hamilton blocked his efforts.

Britain and France went to war in 1793
during the French Revolution. Jefferson and
Hamilton had different thoughts about this too.
Jefferson supported the French Revolution
because he hoped it would lead to a democratic

French government. He wanted France to win its war against the British. Hamilton sided with Great Britain. President Washington finally stepped in. He decided that the United States wouldn't take either side in the fight.

THE RISE OF POLITICAL PARTIES

The different ideas between Hamilton and Jefferson led to something new. Political parties, or groups, formed. Those who agreed with Jefferson called themselves Republicans (they later became the Democratic Party). Jefferson was their leader.

IT'S A FACT!

The disagreements between the Federalists and Republicans grew ugly. At one point, Hamilton printed newspaper articles without signing them. The articles said that Jefferson should be removed from office.

Hamilton and his supporters were called Federalists. President Washington didn't like this idea of political parties. He thought they would tear the nation apart.

Jefferson and John Adams, Washington's vice president, had been close friends since their time together in Paris. But Adams was a Federalist.

Soon politics began to drive them apart. They
disagreed on how the government should be run.
Adams had written a book that criticized the
French Revolution. Jefferson believed strongly in
the ideas that had sparked the revolution. Jefferson
wrote an introduction to a book that criticized
Adams's ideas about the French Revolution.
Jefferson later said that the printer had put that part
in by mistake. But the damage had been done.
Adams was hurt by the words, and their friendship
cooled.

Jefferson hated this division. In 1793, he
resigned as secretary of state. President Washington
begged him to stay, but Jefferson's mind was made
up. He returned to Monticello in January 1794. He
longed for "happiness in the lap and love of my
family, in the society of my neighbors and my
books . . . interest or affection in every bud that
opens, in every breath that blows around me."

Jefferson was safe and happy at Monticello.
But he still kept track of politics. Two events in
1794 bothered him. Farmers in western
Pennsylvania were having a difficult time. They
were deeply in debt. A new tax on whiskey seemed
to be too much. They protested the tax. Some of

Farmers in Pennsylvania protested the tax on whiskey.

them became violent in the Whiskey Rebellion. The government sent an army to crush the protesters. Jefferson was angry. He didn't think that U.S. troops should be used against poor Americans.

Jefferson also disliked a new treaty with the British. Britain still held forts in the United States. British ships were also harassing U.S. ships and sailors. President Washington sent John Jay to Britain to work out a treaty. But the Jay Treaty gave in to the British on almost every point.

Still, Jefferson believed he would enjoy his
home for the rest of his life. In 1795, Patsy's
husband became ill. Jefferson brought their
children to Monticello so Patsy could tend to her
husband. Jefferson loved being surrounded by his
family and breathing the pure air of Monticello.
He spent time on horseback and in the fields. He
worked on new inventions, such as a folding
stool and a life preserver. He built the first swivel
chair. In October 1797, Maria (Polly) Jefferson
married her cousin Jack Eppes at Monticello.

VICE PRESIDENT

In 1796, George Washington announced that he
would not serve a third term as president. The
Federalists nominated John Adams for president.
Jefferson's friend James Madison put in
Jefferson's name as a Republican candidate for
president. Adams won the election and became
the second president of the United States.
Jefferson came in second. According to the law at
that time, this made him vice president.

On March 4, 1799, the fifty-five-year-old
Jefferson went again to Philadelphia, which had
become the nation's capital. As vice president, his

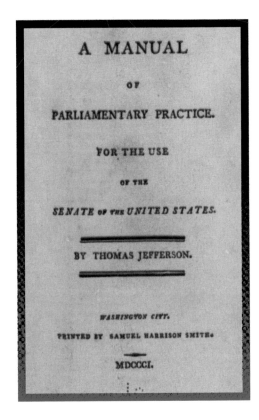

As the vice president, Jefferson's job was to run meetings of the U.S. Senate. He wrote this book of rules to help Senate meetings run smoothly.

only job was to run meetings for the U.S. Senate. The meetings were confusing. Right away, Jefferson wrote a book of rules. The book, *A Manual of Parliamentary Practice,* is still in use.

President Adams was facing problems with the French. The revolution in France had become a massacre. Jefferson believed in the French Revolution. But he didn't want such violence in

America. The Federalists, however, worried that the
revolution could spread to the United States. They
passed a set of laws called the Alien and Sedition
Acts. These laws gave the U.S. president power to
throw out of the country anyone who might be
dangerous. The laws gave the government the right
to arrest writers and newspaper editors who made
statements against the government. Jefferson felt that
these laws went against the freedom of speech
guaranteed in the U.S. Bill of Rights. As vice
president, however, he could not speak out against
Adams's decisions.

In December 1799, George Washington died
at his home in Mount Vernon, Virginia. Many had
thought Washington was the only man who had
worked to bring the political parties together. Some
people said that Jefferson was the person to fill
Washington's shoes. In 1800, the Republicans
again asked Jefferson to run for president against
John Adams.

The campaign was nasty. Jefferson spent this
time quietly at Monticello. He tried to ignore the
articles and cartoons that showed him as a madman.
When the votes were finally counted, Jefferson had
won. He was going to be president.

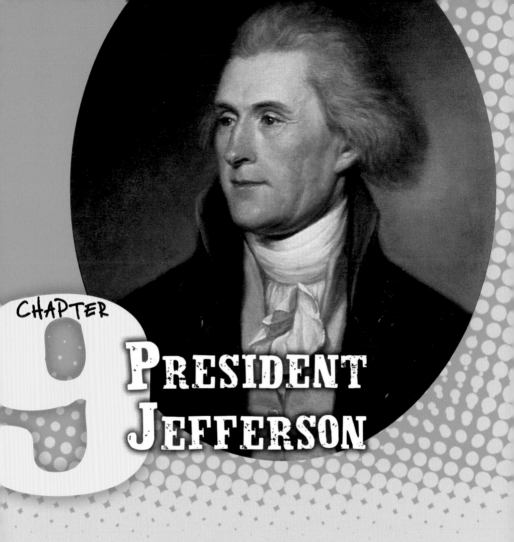

PRESIDENT JEFFERSON

Jefferson was the third president of the United States.

ON MARCH 4, 1801, Thomas Jefferson became the third president of the United States. Aaron Burr, a Republican from New York, was the new vice president.

Jefferson was the first president to take office in Washington, D.C. He had helped design the city. But it wasn't finished yet.

Only a few buildings were done. They were surrounded by mud.

In his inaugural speech, Jefferson talked about the goals of the American Revolution. He promised "equal and exact justice to all men." He also talked about voting and unity. He promised to "do all the good in my power... to the happiness and freedom of all."

IT'S A FACT!

On paper, Jefferson's inaugural address was moving. His delivery, however, was poor. His voice trembled and was hard to hear. Only the people sitting in the first few rows of the crowd could hear him.

Jefferson moved into the new president's home on Pennsylvania Avenue. This building later became known as the White House. The inside of the building wasn't finished. Jefferson had to work in the noise of saws and hammers. But he was used to these sounds from Monticello.

JEFFERSON'S STYLE

Jefferson tried to choose wisely for his cabinet. He picked people from different areas of the country. James Madison of Virginia, Jefferson's close friend and the person he trusted most, became secretary of state. Other cabinet members came from Pennsylvania and other northern states.

Jefferson didn't like to be too formal. He wore plain clothes, even at important dinners. Once he wore his bedroom slippers to meet the British minister. Jefferson believed that all people were equal.

This belief even affected White House dinners. He had all meals served at a round table. That way, no seat would be more important than any other. Instead of having guests come in to dinner in order of their importance, everyone entered together. They took whatever place was available.

IT'S A FACT!

Some White House dinner guests got a special treat. Jefferson served them ice cream made from his own recipe.

The food served at the president's round table was excellent. Jefferson had a skilled chef who made French and Italian foods. These

REMEMBERING NATIVE AMERICANS

A Cherokee chief, Ontassete, was a friend of Jefferson's father Peter. Jefferson later wrote about a boyhood visit with the chief. "His voice...and the solemn silence of the people at their [camp] fires filled me with awe." These visits impressed young Tom. One of his favorite activities was exploring abandoned Indian villages and collecting arrowheads. Later in life, he often supported the rights of Native Americans.

included pancakes and macaroni, both of which were new to most Americans.

All people were welcomed to the president's house. At a Fourth of July party, Jefferson talked with diplomats, farmers, senators, and clerks. He enjoyed a pleasant talk with several Native American chiefs. He tried to improve his use of the Cherokee language.

One of Jefferson's first acts as president was to pardon, or release, everyone who had been jailed under the Alien and Sedition Acts. He sent personal letters of apology to people who had been arrested. Next, he removed many taxes that the government had placed on its people, including the whiskey tax. He also sent ships to

War with Tripoli

Thomas Jefferson was president when the United States fought its first war since the American Revolution. The war was with the Barbary States, small states on the northern coast of Africa that were home to many pirates. These Barbary pirates attacked and robbed ships on the high seas. The pirates were greatly feared. Many nations, including the United States, paid the pirates to keep away from their ships.

Jefferson did not think the United States should pay pirates. In 1801, one of the Barbary States, Tripoli, demanded more money. Jefferson refused. On May 14, 1801, the ruler of Tripoli declared war on the United States. Jefferson sent U.S. Navy warships commanded by Admiral Edward Preble to block the port of Tripoli. The pirates captured one of the U.S. ships, the *Philadelphia*. They dragged off the sailors and jailed them. Then the pirates put their own crew aboard and bragged that they owned a U.S. ship. Under the cover of night, Stephen Decatur, a young U.S. naval officer, sailed a small boat into Tripoli harbor and set the *Philadelphia* on fire. Decatur became a hero for his daring action.

North Africa in response to attacks on U.S. ships by pirates.

Jefferson was against many programs started by Alexander Hamilton, including the national bank. Still, Jefferson left many of these programs in place. He didn't want to anger his opponents too much. On one issue, however, he felt strongly. A large national debt had been built up under Hamilton. Jefferson promised to pay off as much of this debt as possible.

THE LOUISIANA PURCHASE

Jefferson saw that the boundaries of the young United States were slowly moving westward. He was in favor of expansion of the country's land. One area to the west was called the Louisiana Territory. This land belonged to France. It covered more than one million square miles of forests, plains, mountains, and river valleys in North America.

The territory stretched from the Mississippi River west and north to the Rocky Mountains. Americans hadn't explored much of the area, but it included the city of New Orleans. New Orleans was near the border separating Louisiana from the United States. The city had an important port on the Mississippi River. Some U.S leaders feared having the port city controlled by the French and their new ruler, Napoleon Bonaparte.

In 1803, Jefferson sent James Monroe to Paris to try to buy New Orleans for $10 million. Napoleon needed money. To everyone's surprise,

Napoleon Bonaparte ruled France from 1799 to 1815.

Napoleon agreed to sell all of the Louisiana Territory to the United States for $15 million. With the Louisiana Purchase, Jefferson had doubled the size of the United States. Americans were excited. Celebrations were held all around the country. Jefferson called the new territory an addition to "the empire of liberty" and a "widespread field for the blessings of liberty."

People wondered what was in this new land. No one was more curious than Jefferson himself. Right away, he started to set up a group to explore the area. Jefferson had taught his secretary, Captain Meriwether Lewis, skills such as mapmaking, surveying, and how to identify plants and wildlife. He chose Lewis to be one of the expedition's leaders. A soldier, Captain William Clark, would be another leader. Lewis and Clark were to travel up the Mississippi River to the point where it joined with the Missouri River. From there, their job was to try to find a water route west to the Pacific Ocean.

This map shows the route of the Lewis and Clark expedition, called the Corps of Discovery.

LEWIS AND CLARK EXPEDITION

With the Louisiana Purchase, the United States gained a huge new piece of land. There were many legends about the area. People told stories about mountains of salt and seven-foot-tall beavers. Jefferson sent Meriwether Lewis and William Clark and a team of men they called the Corps of Discovery to explore the West. Jefferson told Lewis and Clark to survey the land and keep a record of plants, animals, rivers, and mountains they saw. He wanted them to observe the people who lived there. He asked them to note the details of native languages and customs. But the main goal was to find a water route to the Pacific Ocean.

The Corps of Discovery set out from Saint Louis, Missouri, on May 21, 1804. The team of forty-eight men included hunters, soldiers, and boatmen. They traveled up the Missouri River. After covering 1,400 miles, cold weather forced them to stop in what would become North Dakota. There, they spent the winter with Mandans, a Native American group.

William Clark

Meriwether Lewis

The following spring, they set off again up the Missouri River into Montana. A Canadian trapper named Toussaint Charbonneau and his Shoshone wife, Sacagawea, joined the group. With her small child strapped to her back, she guided them through dangerous lands. At one point, when they were out of food and supplies, Sacagawea asked a group of Shoshone Indians to help the explorers.

Lewis and Clark found that there was no water passage from the Mississippi River to the Pacific. Instead, they had to walk through deep snow on narrow trails. Sacagawea's Shoshone friends gave them horses to cross the Rocky Mountains. On the other side of the mountains, they paddled down the Columbia River. On November 15, 1805, the explorers finally saw the Pacific Ocean. They spent the winter there and in spring began the return journey.

During the trip, the Corps of Discovery recorded 122 animals and 178 plants and trees that were new to them. They wrote of bison, elk and deer, and a creature they called a "cabic" (a pronghorn). They told how Captain Clark killed a huge brown bear that was almost nine feet tall. The Corps of Discovery were the first Americans to see grizzly bears. Their records describe prairie dogs that lived in villages of their own and black-footed ferrets that also roamed the prairies.

Lewis and Clark were welcomed as heroes when they returned. They had not found a water route to the Pacific. But they had mapped and opened up the western United States for future settlers.

A SECOND TERM

Jefferson ran for reelection in 1804. He was a popular president and easily won the election. George Clinton, governor of New York, became vice president.

Just before his second election, in April 1804, Jefferson rushed home to Monticello to see his twenty-five-year-old daughter, Maria. Maria had been ill following childbirth. Jefferson arrived just in time to see her once more before she died. It seemed as if tragedy would forever haunt the Jefferson family. "My loss is great," he wrote. "I have lost even the half of all I had."

Jefferson's second term as president was less successful than the first. He faced many challenges. A political enemy publicly accused Jefferson of fathering the children of one of his slaves, Sally Hemings. Jefferson denied the accusation. (Modern scientific evidence shows that one of the Hemings family ancestors was indeed a member of the Jefferson family. Some people think it was a Jefferson nephew who fathered the children. Others believe it was Thomas Jefferson himself.)

Some Americans also were unhappy with how Jefferson was dealing with the British. British soldiers were boarding U.S. ships at sea. They forced U.S.

British sailors attack a U.S. ship. They hope to force some U.S. sailors to fight with them against the French.

sailors to fight with them against the French. Jefferson wanted to avoid war. So he said that the United States would refuse to trade with Britain.

Jefferson thought this action would hurt the British. But it hurt U.S. businesses more. Business owners turned against the president. Articles and cartoons attacking him appeared in newspapers. Finally, Jefferson gave in to the pressure and allowed U.S. businesses to trade with Great Britain once more.

By the time his second term was over in 1809, Jefferson was glad to be leaving public life. "Never did a prisoner, released from his chains, feel such relief as I shall on shaking off the shackles of power."

Jefferson's party wanted him to run again. But he followed George Washington's example and left office after two terms. He looked forward to returning to a happier life at Monticello.

CHAPTER

10 THE FINAL YEARS

Jefferson left Washington in 1809. He spent the rest of his life at Monticello (above).

FOR MUCH OF HIS LIFE, duty to his country had kept Jefferson away from Monticello. "Nature intended me for the tranquil pursuits of science," he wrote. "But the enormities of the times in which I have lived have forced me to take a part." At the age of sixty-five, he could look forward to spending the rest of his days at his beloved home.

His first job was to complete Monticello. Jefferson planned the final details, including horseback-riding trails, orchards, and gardens. He chose paint colors and curtains. He decided where to put paintings, maps, and other objects. He enjoyed the time he had to read and study. His library grew to a huge size. Jefferson later gave the books to the U.S. government. They became part of the Library of Congress, the nation's biggest library, in Washington, D.C.

The Library of Congress has more than 500 miles of bookshelves. They hold more than 126 million items.

MONTICELLO

Monticello is located in Albemarle County, Virginia, near the city of Charlottesville. At first, Jefferson planned for the home to have fourteen rooms. As time passed, he continued to add to the plans. Thirty-nine years after it was started, the building was completed. It had forty-three rooms.

Jefferson invented a ceiling compass for his home that connected to a weather vane on the roof. The invention allowed him to tell the strength and direction of the wind from inside the house. A clock in the hall is operated by cannonball weights. It shows the day of the week as well as the time. Jefferson also designed a lifting system called a dumbwaiter to bring wine up from the cellar. He added a revolving door between the kitchen and the dining room. Monticello had five privies (bathrooms). Two were inside, which was unusual for the time. Most bathrooms were outdoors.

The style of the main house at Monticello is called neoclassical because it is based on ancient Greek and Roman designs. It is made of red brick trimmed with white wood. A white dome rises above the house. In front is a porch with tall columns.

Jefferson was more than $107,000 in debt when he died in 1826. His only surviving daughter, Martha, had to sell the house. The new owner didn't care for it very well. The home was slowly becoming a ruin. But Uriah P. Levy, a naval officer who admired Jefferson, visited Monticello in 1834. He was sad to see the poor condition of the home. Levy bought Monticello and repaired it. He believed it should be a national monument. He planned to donate it to the American people. Before that could happen, the Civil War (1861–1865) started. Southern forces took over Monticello. It was not returned to the Levy family until 1879. Uriah P. Levy's nephew and his family spent millions of dollars to preserve the house. In 1923, the Levy family sold it to the Thomas Jefferson Foundation. Both the house and plantation have been restored and are open to the public.

DAILY LIFE

The "sage [wise man] of Monticello" wrote to many
people. He wrote to the new president, James
Madison, and to other government leaders. He also
wrote to his old friend, John Adams. After years of
political disagreement, the two began their
friendship again. They discussed politics, religion,
and many other subjects. Jefferson also wrote to
family, friends, and interesting people around the
world. During his lifetime, he wrote nearly twenty
thousand letters.

Jefferson wrote in a small office that he called
his cabinet. He was surrounded by his own
inventions, including a revolving book stand and
his polygraph machine. He always worked at the
same time each day. Everyone knew he must not
be bothered during these hours.

Jefferson's daughter Martha lived at Monticello.
The home was always filled with the people he
loved—his children, grandchildren, nieces, nephews,
and other family members. They gathered in the
evenings for games and music. Sometimes Jefferson
played the violin while his grandchildren danced
around him. Many evenings were spent reading.
The children followed their grandfather's example

and read quietly. One of his granddaughters remembered, "He talked with us affectionately . . . our small follies [faults] he treated with good humor . . . our graver ones with kind . . . admonition [scolding]. . . . I used to . . . sit on his knee and play with his watch chain. I loved and honored him above all earthly beings."

A constant flow of visitors came to Monticello. It was not unusual for twenty or more guests to come for breakfast. They were served tea, coffee, muffins, ham, and warm corn bread. People came from all over the world. They toured Monticello, admiring its charm and beauty. They watched as Jefferson showed off his inventions. They discussed the latest news of the country and the world.

LAST DAYS

Thomas Jefferson always believed that free public education was important for democracy. He spent years developing his ideas for a public university. He decided on classes, types of teachers, and classroom design. He even drew up plans for a building. In 1825, Jefferson's dream came true when the University of Virginia opened. It was

not just a college for the wealthy. Poor students
who showed talent went to classes for free.

Thomas Jefferson
lived to see the fiftieth
anniversary of his country.
He died at Monticello on
Independence Day, July 4,
1826, at the age of 83.

Jefferson had
prepared the words for his
gravestone. It listed what
he thought of as his most
important achievements.

IT'S A FACT!

Jefferson's old friend
John Adams died on
the same day as
Jefferson, July 4,
1826. This was the
fiftieth anniversary
of the Declaration of
Independence.

Here was buried Thomas Jefferson
Author of the Declaration of Independence
Of the Statute of Virginia for religious
   toleration
& Father of the University of Virginia

More than one hundred years after Jefferson's
death, the U.S. Congress agreed to build a
national monument to honor him. The Thomas
Jefferson Memorial was completed in 1943. It is
located in East Potomac Park in Washington, D.C.

The Thomas Jefferson Memorial in Washington, D.C.

John Russell Pope designed the Roman-style white marble building to honor Jefferson's love of classical architecture. Twenty-six columns form a circle covered by a domed ceiling. Steps lead to a bronze statue of Jefferson. The statue is nineteen feet tall. A panel below the dome bears Jefferson's words: "I have sworn upon the altar of God eternal hostility against every form of tyranny over the mind of man."

Quotations from the Declaration of Independence and from Jefferson's other writings are also on the marble panels. These words about freedom and democracy show the ideas upon which the United States and all democracies have been built and are a fitting way to honor the nation's third president.

Barbary State: one of the areas along the Barbary Coast of North Africa. The states were Algiers, Morocco, Tripoli, and Tunis. In the 1800s, they were together known as the Barbary States.

Bill of Rights: the first ten amendments (changes or additions) to the U.S. Constitution. These amendments limit the power of the U.S. government and protect the rights and freedoms of individuals.

boycott: to stop buying or taking part in something as a way of protesting to force change

British Parliament: the lawmaking body in the British government

British rule: Britain ruled many colonies around the world. It had colonies in Asia, Africa, North America, and South America and claimed the entire continent of Australia. Most of these colonies became free of British rule in the 1900s.

colony: a territory set up by a country that is far away. In the 1600s and 1700s, Britain set up thirteen colonies along the eastern coast of what would become the United States.

congress: a formal meeting of people to set policies or make laws. During and after the American Revolution, several congresses met. Jefferson went to the First and Second Continental Congresses.

Constitutional Convention: the meeting in 1787 to write the U.S. Constitution

Corps of Discovery: the expedition led by Meriwether Lewis and William Clark to explore the Louisiana Territory, which the United States had bought in 1803

Federalist: in Jefferson's time, a member of a U.S. political party that favored a strong U.S. central government

Louisiana Purchase: a huge area that covered the middle of the United States, which the new nation bought from France in 1803

neoclassical: new designs that were based on the art and style of ancient Greece and ancient Rome

plantation: a large farm. In the 1700s and up to the mid-1800s, plantations in the southern United States typically used slave labor.

Republican: in Jefferson's time, a member of a U.S. political party that favored a weak U.S. central government, with more authority in the hands of the states

scientific method: an organized set of rules—of seeing, of forming explanations, and of testing those explanations—to find the answers to scientific questions

Sons of Liberty: a group of American colonists who fought secretly against British rule in the late 1700s

SOURCE NOTES

9 Sarah N. Randolph, *The Domestic Life of Thomas Jefferson* (Cambridge: MA: University Press, 1947), 4.

14 Claude G. Bowers, *The Young Jefferson* (Boston: Houghton Mifflin, 1969), 14.

16 Randolph, 12.

16 Ibid.

17 Ibid.

17 Ibid., 13.

17 Ibid., 12.

18 Bowers, 21.

18 Randolph, 12.

23 Fawn M. Brodie, *Thomas Jefferson: An Intimate History* (New York: W. W. Norton, 1974), 39, 69.

24 Ibid., 72.

25 Ibid.

30 Bowers, 45.

33 Ibid., 47.

34 E. M. Halliday, *Understanding Thomas Jefferson* (New York: HarperCollins, 2001), 32.

35 Brodie, 86.

37 Randolph, 28.

42 A. J. Langguth, *Patriots: The Men Who Started the American Revolution* (New York: Touchstone/Simon & Schuster, 1988), 69.

44 Brodie, 108–109.

47 Ibid., 111.

47 Ibid., 115.

48 Bowers, 148.

49 *Encyclopaedia Britannica,* 14th ed., s.v. "Declaration of Independence."

49 Ibid.

50 Langguth, 307.

51 American Heritage Publishing, *Thomas Jefferson and His World* (New York: American Heritage Publishing, 1960), 53.

52 Bowers, 212.

55 Randolph, 35.

56 Brodie, 149.

59 Ibid., 161.

59 Ibid., 157.

59 Ibid., 152.

60 Ibid., 153.

61 Randolph, 40.

61 Ibid., 41–42.

62 Ibid.

62 Bowers, 311.

66 Page Smith, *John Adams* (New York: Doubleday, 1962), 625.

79 Brodie, 263

76 Randolph, 116.

76 Ibid., 496.

77 Brodie, 263.

85 Willard Sterne Randall, *Thomas Jefferson: A Life* (New York: Henry Holt & Co., 1993), 548.

85 Randolph, 235.

90 Randall, 567.

94 Randolph, 257.

95 Ibid., 278.

96 William J. Bennett, ed., *Our Sacred Honor* (New York: Simon & Schuster, 1997), 222.

100 Randolph, 295.

101 Randall, 595.

102 Halliday, 239.

SELECTED BIBLIOGRAPHY

American Heritage Publishing. *Thomas Jefferson and His World*. New York: American Heritage Publishing, 1960.

Bennett, William J., ed. *Our Sacred Honor*. New York: Simon & Schuster, 1997.

Bowers, Claude G. *The Young Jefferson*. Boston: Houghton Mifflin, 1969.

Brodie, Fawn M. *Thomas Jefferson: An Intimate History*. New York: W. W. Norton, 1974.

Ellis, Joseph J. *Founding Brothers*. New York: Alfred A. Knopf, 2000.

Favorite Jefferson Quotes. 2002. http://etext.virginia.edu/jefferson/quotations/jeffl.htm

Fleming, Thomas. *The Man from Monticello: An Intimate Life of Thomas Jefferson*. New York: William Morrow & Co., 1969.

Halliday, E. M. *Understanding Thomas Jefferson*. New York, HarperCollins, 2001.

Langguth, A. J. *Patriots: The Men Who Started the American Revolution*. New York: Touchstone/Simon & Schuster, 1988.

Malone, Dumas. *Jefferson the Virginian*. Boston: Little, Brown, & Co., 1948.

McLaughlin, Jack. *Jefferson and Monticello*. New York: Henry Holt & Co., 1988.

Randall, Willard Sterne. *Thomas Jefferson: A Life*. New York: Henry Holt & Co., 1993.

Randolph, Sarah N. *The Domestic Life of Thomas Jefferson*. Cambridge, MA: University Press, 1947.

Shorto, Russell. *Thomas Jefferson and the American Ideal*. Hauppauge, NY: Barron's, 1987.

FURTHER READING AND WEBSITES

Bober, Natalie S. *Thomas Jefferson: Man on a Mountain*. New York: Atheneum, 1999.

Bowen, Andy Russell. *The Back of Beyond: A Story about Lewis and Clark*. Minneapolis: Carolrhoda Books, Inc., 1997.

Day, Nancy. *Your Travel Guide to Colonial America*. Minneapolis: Lerner Publications Company, 2001.

Erdrich, Lise. *Sacagawea*. Minneapolis: Carolrhoda Books, Inc., 2003.

Ferris, Jeri Chase. *Thomas Jefferson: Father of Liberty*. Minneapolis: Carolrhoda Books, Inc., 1998.

Hakim, Jay. *From Colonies to Country*. New York: Oxford University Press, 1999.

Miller, Brandon Marie. *Growing Up in Revolution and the New Nation (1774–1800)*. Minneapolis: Lerner Publications Company, 2003.

Monticello: The Home of Thomas Jefferson. http://www.Monticello.org. This site has information about Jefferson and virtual tours of the house and gardens.

Shanger, Rosalyn. *How We Crossed the West: The Adventures of Lewis and Clark*. Washington, DC: National Geographic, 1997.

Streissguth, Tom. *Benjamin Franklin*. Minneapolis: Lerner Publications Company, 2005.

Swain. Gwenyth. *Declaring Freedom: A Look at the Declaration of Independence, the Bill of Rights, and the Constitution*. Minneapolis: Lerner Publications Company, 2004.

Thomas Jefferson Digital Archive. http://etext.virginia.edu/jefferson. This site offers Jefferson papers, a biography, selected quotations, and the history of Jefferson's plans for the University of Virginia.

Young, Robert. *A Personal Tour of Monticello*. Minneapolis: Lerner Publications Company, 1999.

PHOTO ACKNOWLEDGMENTS

The images in this book are used with the permission of: © North Wind Picture Archives, pp. 4, 15, 39, 51, 55, 70, 73, 74, 80, 92 (both); Laura Westlund, pp. 7, 91; Monticello/Thomas Jefferson Foundation, Inc., pp. 10, 35, 46, 72; Independent Picture Service, pp. 13, 45 (left), 90; Library of Congress, pp. 17 (top) [LC-MSS-27748-64] (bottom), 22 (Thomas Jefferson Papers Series 5. Commonplace Books), 27 (LC-USZ61-536), 41 (LC-USZC4-523), 42 (LC-USZ62-3775), 58 (Thomas Jefferson Papers Series 1. General Correspondence, 1651-1827), 82 (Thomas Jefferson Papers Series 7. Miscellaneous Bound Volumes), 96 (LC-H812-T-M09-007-A), 97 (HABS,DC,WASH,461A-26), 102 (LC-USE6-D-010109); Massachusetts Historical Society, pp. 25, 31; National Archives, p. 45 (right); Peter Newark's American Pictures, p. 53; Architect of the Capitol, p. 57; © The Art Archive/Musée Carnavalet Paris/Dagli Orti (A), p. 63; © Buddy Mays/Travel Stock, p. 68; Independence National Historical Park, p. 84; The Mariners' Museum, Newport News, VA, p. 95

Front Cover: © Bettmann/CORBIS